MW01148286

Managing Friends & Former Peers

By Gary Winters
San Diego, California

One of the *Just In Time* Leadership Series

See the full series at
www.justintimeleadershiptips.com

© 2013 All Rights Reserved

What Readers Are Saying

"I read *Managing Friends and Former Peers* on a one-hour flight. The book is short, sweet, and jam-packed with tips and techniques to manage this potentially delicate dynamic."

Sommer Kerhlie, San Diego, California

"This book was indeed "Just In Time" for me, given my recent promotion. I read it with anticipation, and it didn't disappoint. It's quite easy to read, even while exploring topics that can be daunting. The conversations with Lisa and Scott are spot-on, offering practical examples of how to flesh out the principles of the book. *Managing Friends & Former Peers* is a winner!"

Wesley Virnelson, Parma, Ohio

"This book was extremely informative and right on point. I love how it tackles just one subject in a format that's both easy to read and easy to apply. My only regret is that I didn't have *Managing Friends & Former Peers* when I first began my transition from "friendco" to manager."

Christina Schone, San Diego, California

Author Online!

For updates and more resources, visit Gary Winters' webpage and *Leadership Almanac* blog at:

www.garywinters.com

Copyright © 2013 by Gary Winters

All rights reserved. No part of this book may be reproduced or transmitted in any form or by any means, electronic or mechanical, including photocopying, recording, or by any information storage and retrieval system, without permission in writing from the copyright owner.

Managing Friends & Former Peers

By Gary Winters
San Diego, California

To Mom and Dad

Married for nearly 67 years;
you left to dance in heaven in 2010.
This one's for you.

About the Author

Gary Winters has worked with scores of leaders over the past 25 years in all kinds of organizations – large, small, in both the public and the private sector. Based in San Diego and available nationwide, his services include:

- One on one coaching
- Team building
- Leadership workshops and academies (design and delivery)
- Keynote speaking

Gary created *The Leadership Almanac* in 2008, a blog where you'll find dozens of articles with practical wisdom about the art of leadership.

Other books by Gary Winters include:

- *How to Manage the Soon-to-Retire Employee*
- *So, How Was Your Meeting?*
- *To Do or Not To Do–How Successful Leaders Make Better Decisions* (with Eric Klein)

Contact information:

Web: www.garywinters.com

Email: gary@garywinters.com

Phone: 619.840.0148

Table of Contents

Welcome to the "Just in Time" Series

Welcome! If this is your first *Just In Time* book, let me tell you about the rationale and philosophy behind this series. If you've already read one or more of the series, skip this introduction and go to this book's introduction which follows.

I've spent nearly three decades in leadership development - as a coach, a workshop facilitator, and a seminar designer. I have delivered hundreds of programs to thousands of people. I've had the privilege of working with highly talented co-facilitators and attending powerful workshops designed and delivered by others. I love leadership development and am proud to have had an impact on so many people.

Leadership training offers many benefits to participants. The presenter is a subject matter expert who brings experience and knowledge of each content area to the table. Good facilitators also have a deep understanding of how adults learn, and strive to make their programs interactive, informative, and even fun. Gathering with other participants can be invaluable, as you can share experiences, build a network of colleagues, and come to understand that others share your concerns and questions. Only in training programs such as these can participants practice skills in a hands-on way, through role-plays, case studies, and simulations. Another plus for formal training is that you can ask specific questions about issues you're dealing with back home, and get suggestions and tips from both the program facilitator and fellow participants.

But, there's one big problem with most leadership training.

Timing.

Too often, leadership development activities occur well *before*, or well *after* you need to apply particular skills that were presented in the workshop.

Suppose you've come to realize you need to start coaching a marginal performer - something you haven't done before. Perhaps you've had the good fortune of leading a team of steady performers who consistently meet (and occasionally exceed) the standards, goals and objectives you've set for the team.

But lately, Tom's performance is has been spotty. His absenteeism is up. He seems lethargic and disengaged. He's starting to miss deadlines and comes to staff meetings late - and has little to say.

You need to do something. You need to talk with Tom. You need to find out what's going on, and what can be done to bring Tom back to his former level of performance.

You know what you *want* to do, but you are not sure *how* to do it.

Perhaps you attended a terrific leadership academy six or eight months ago, which left you feeling energized, enthusiastic, and with a very "full brain." You came back to work with a renewed commitment to put dozens of ideas into practice.

But much of the content presented at the seminar may not have been on your plate since then. You haven't had to conduct a performance review; you haven't had to deliver a technical presentation to a non-technical audience, or you haven't been put in charge of a new team.

You remember the topic of interest to you now (coaching a marginal performer) was discussed at the academy - but how much do you remember of the presentation? Anything? Ten percent? Twenty?

Sadly, your memory loss is typical.

Most of us begin to forget much of what we've learned in leadership training almost immediately, unless we're using those skills right away. Within a few weeks, many of the insights, awareness, and techniques you could use to enhance your upcoming coaching experience have been filed in forgotten corners of your brain. They're in there somewhere - but you can't recall them.

What can you do?

· You could wing it and hope for the best. Perhaps, as you start coaching, the suggestions and guidelines you learned in the classroom will come back to you. Then again, perhaps not.

· You could pull out the handouts or the workbook that came with the seminar (if you still have them and can find them). However, for the most part you're likely to find some PowerPoint slides, or some "key points" in a workbook with your own handwritten notes. They may jog your memory a bit - but probably not enough.

· You could search for a conventional book on the topic - but who has time (or the desire) to read 240 pages on *Everything You Need to Know to Coach Employees*, and then extract what's useful for your situation.

On the other hand, perhaps you *haven't* attended a leadership academy. Now it's not a matter of forgetting much of what you've learned - it's a matter of not knowing in the first place.

You have the dilemma of wanting to apply a skill you haven't learned, and the odds are high that while there are seminars and workshops available that address your need, they are scheduled weeks or months in the future.

Whether you've attended leadership training and want to get back "up to speed" on some of the content, or you need to address an issue well before you can attend an appropriate training, you want to do something *right now*.

What you need is a resource that's specific to your concern, practical, and action-oriented (rather than simply thought-provoking). You need something which hits the sweet spot between a one page handout and a volume of two- or three-hundred pages.

You need a *Just In Time* book - like the one you're reading now.

The *Just In Time* Leadership Series is an ever-expanding catalogue of books that cover topics of interest to managers, supervisors, team leaders - just about anyone who coordinates and directs a group of people. These books are meant to be read "just in time" - that is, just before you are about to do something that leaders do: conduct an interview, facilitate a cross-sectional team meeting, create annual team and individual goals, reward and recognize a high performer, or whatever it might be.

Just In Time books close the gap between the workshop and the application. They are not intended to replace formal learning events (or mentoring, for that matter) - they are designed to assist you *before* or *after* those events. They will bring you "up to speed" on with the techniques and insights associated with leadership competencies. They are stuffed with proven TIPS (Techniques, Insight, and Practical Solutions) associated with skills that leaders need to be effective.

They do this just in time.

All *Just In Time* books share some common characteristics:

- They are written in casual, non-technical language. Reading one is something like having a cup of coffee with a leadership coach.

- They are brief but thorough. Longer than an article, but considerably shorter than a textbook. You could read one in an hour or so.

- They focus on insights *and* techniques. Insights give you the "why," and techniques show you "how." These books will help you think and act.

- Each *Just In Time* book covers just one topic. You could attend a full-day program on performance coaching, but soon have to do something quite specific: handle office gossip, or council an employee who's going through a personal challenge, or set some new ground rules with an employee you now supervise who's been your friend and peer for the last four years. There's a *Just In Time* book for each of these - or will be soon!

- *Just In Time* books won't break the pocketbook, either. That workshop you attended (or will attend) could cost hundreds of dollars. A *Just In Time* ebook is about the price of a cup of coffee.

Once again, welcome to the *Just In Time* leadership series. I'm confident the book you're now reading will provide insights and techniques that will give you the confidence to deal effectively with the leadership challenge that you face today.

Warm regards,

Gary Winters

Phone:	619.840.0148
Email:	gary@garywinters.com
Web:	www.garywinters.com

What Have You Gotten Yourself Into?

Managing friends, former peers or co-workers is rarely easy when you first become their manager.

Most of the time, people find themselves in this awkward situation when they are promoted to a leadership role in their current department. It can also happen when someone who's been your friend, colleague or peer transfers into your department and now reports to you.

Sometimes, you're asked to manage someone who's been your personal friend for a some time. You have a history together beyond the workplace, where you share mutual interests. You could be members of the same social circle outside work.

Sometimes, the colleague you now manage is someone you've known only at work. You might lunch together frequently. This could be a co-worker you've taken into your confidence when you wanted to talk about problems at work - or even your old boss.

Whether close personal friend or familiar co-worker, there's a bond, a relationship with some history and a set of expectations of one another.

When you become the boss, everything about these relationships can suddenly be uncomfortable. There's a new set of groundrules to establish - as the manager, you are going be held accountable for the work performance of any friends or former co-workers on the team, and they are going to have to come to terms with the fact that they now report to you. *Everyone* involved can feel awkward and hesitant about the future.

Managing personal friends is tricky, in part, because you may want to sustain the relationship while succeeding in your new job.

With former co-workers, there can be other issues at play. If you're taking charge of your current department, there could be people who:

- Wanted the promotion given to you.
- Feel you're not qualified for the job.
- Deeply miss your predecessor and resent having to "start over" with someone else.

- Expect special treatment from you based on the connection you had as peers.

As the new manager, you will have a million things on your mind, from big stuff such as...

- Managing your own transition into your new role
- Building a good relationship with your new boss
- Establishing your credibility and expectations with your new team

...to practical stuff, like...

- Preparing the budget for the next quarter
- Conducting interviews for new employees
- Reviewing new policies and procedures
- And so on

The transition into management is challenging under any circumstances. Doing so when one or more members of the team are personal friends or former peers can be daunting. That said, it can be done. This book will give you what you need to know to move forward with confidence and grace.

(By the way, for the purposes of a bit of shorthand, so I won't have to use the rather awkward phrase "friends or former peers" throughout the book, I've coined a word:

friendcos. "Friendcos" are either personal friends, former co-workers and colleagues, or both. Friend + Co - get it?)

This *Just In Time* ebook is focused on just one aspect of management - *how to manage friendcos*, a niche leadership skill which is a subset of broader leadership competencies - holding difficult conversations, coaching employees, and setting standards, to name a few. We're going to put a microscope on one very important skill - managing friendcos.

You *can* successfully manage people who've been your friend or co-worker. It won't happen by chance, and it's not a matter of pulling some management "trick" out of your hat. But you *can* learn how to do it, and you can apply what you're about to learn right away.

Let's start your new leadership assignment with confidence.

CHAPTER ONE

Will They Support, Sabotage, or Split?

W hen you boil it down, there are really only three kinds of employees: those who **support** you, those who **sabotage** you, and those who are so burned out or unmotivated they need to **split**.

The good news? Most people are supportive.

If you lead well, people will follow. You can have a staff of very supportive folks, who believe in you, share your passion for the team's mission, and are committed to making a difference with their work.

Supporters can be counted on to fully engage in the operation. They meet their responsibilities, accept accountability for their performance, look for ways to do their jobs more effectively, and make an effort to be a good team player.

This is not to say they won't have bad days, won't have strong and sometimes contrary opinions, or won't challenge your decisions from time to time. They will - but they will do so with a spirit of contribution, of engagement, of heart.

Some people choose to sabotage.

Sometimes people decide they can't - or won't - support their leader (or the organization). Their behavior becomes a form of sabotage. If they're giving less than what they're capable of giving, they're sabotaging the mission.

It's a strong word. But think about it - members of your new team will either be working *for* you, or they'll be working *against* you. They're either *helping* or *hurting* the cause. They're either *productive* or *counter-productive*. There's no Switzerland here - no neutral ground.

The kind of employee sabotage you're likely to encounter is subtle. It's not the workplace violence that makes the 6 o'clock news.

It begins when people feel they have no other option. They no longer feel supportive. They're fed up. Maybe they're disappointed being told an expected salary increase didn't happen - again. Or they're completely disillusioned with the mantra, "Let's do more with less." Maybe they feel they've been placed in the middle of an ethical dilemma. Whatever the reason, they have lost faith in you, as their leader, or the organization as a whole. They won't, or can't, continue to be a supporter.

Why don't they just quit if things are so bad? Maybe it's a tough job market. Maybe they're too close to retirement. Maybe they have any of a hundred good reasons. Who knows?

They stay on the job, but feel powerless to change whatever's pulling them down. The job becomes something they *have* to do rather than what they *want* to do - and that produces tension. Engaging in sabotage (even if it's largely non-conscious behavior) is a way of releasing that tension. As they say, *Don't get mad, get even!*

Sabotage takes many forms. One is called *malicious compliance*, which happens when a person does *exactly* what they're told to do - but nothing more.

If someone wants to sabotage a leader or the organization, how they do so is constrained only by their imagination.

- They could pretend to agree with a consensus-based decision and then bad-mouth it afterwards with their co-workers.

· They could work on an assignment, spot an opportunity to make a process improvement, and do nothing about it.

· They could remain silent in staff meetings, contributing nothing to the discussions.

· They could start leaving work at "quitting time" every day, regardless of what's going on or whether they could complete an important task if they stayed a few minutes longer.

Choosing to **not** "give it your best" is a powerful form of sabotage.

Some people choose to split.

They actually quit. They find a better opportunity somewhere else. That's fine if they are poor performers, but it's costly when they're valued members of the team.

What has this to do with supervising friendcos?

If you have personal friends on your new staff, it's safe to assume that they have been among your most loyal supporters. That's something close friends do for one each other.

But when you become their manager, that desire to be supportive can be fragile. When a friend becomes the boss, there's been a shift in the power balance that can't be ignored (even if it isn't discussed). Unless you handle the change in your relationship with grace, you can both find yourselves in a difficult situation, confused, unsure how to proceed, stuck.

That's not to say your friends are destined to become deliberate saboteurs. But during the transition, as you become their boss and they become your subordinate, they may not be able to give 100% to their responsibilities while they sort out what all this will mean for them. This is not *deliberate* sabotage, but it's behavior that has costs for the team and organization nonetheless.

And then there's your former co-workers, who now work *for* you.

They *might* be your ally, but they could just as easily sabotage your efforts to establish yourself as the new leader because they don't believe you *should* be the new leader. Don't assume they will be loyal supporters by default. Regardless of how well you worked together before you took charge, they may have strong feelings about your promotion for any number of reasons (they wanted the job; they think you're unqualified; they wanted someone else to get the job; they miss the previous manager, etc.).

Your success depends on your ability to build and inspire a team of people, *including friendcos*, who genuinely support you. It defaults to *you* to be proactive about clarifying your expectations and setting the ground rules for the new relationship - manager/subordinate - because *you* are in charge. You're the leader.

Ignoring the issue, by the way, doesn't make it go away. It becomes the elephant in the room. (Or is it the 800 pound gorilla?) Hoping things will work out on their own won't cut it. Relying on the strength and history of the relationship to convince yourself that everything will be fine during this fundamental change in your career is being foolish.

If you want to succeed as the manager, there is no real alternative to consciously, deliberately, and immediately engaging all the friendcos in a process to transform the relationship.

Avoiding your discomfort can quickly turn would-be supporters into saboteurs. They need your leadership to transform and embrace a new relationship with you. You both need to take a journey of transition.

CHAPTER TWO

The Inner Game of Transition

Becoming a manager is a big change in your life. You'll have more responsibilities, bigger challenges, and fresh opportunities. For those in your department, it means fundamental changes as well.

We need to distinguish between *change* and *transition*. Author and organizational consultant William Bridges defines change as something that happens *to* you, while transition is something that happens *within* you.

Change is external, observable and public. It starts with the *new beginning* and can be pin-pointed to a specific date. Change is *the next big thing*. When the change is thought to be positive, it is associated with words like new, bigger, smaller, better, faster, cheaper, or more effective.

Transition, by contrast, begins with an *ending*. It starts when you begin *letting go*. It's not tied to a specific date but rather it concludes when you have the awareness that you've *arrived* (a phase called the *new beginning*). Change is instant, but transition takes time. Starting a transition is associated with words like loss, giving up, letting go, leaving behind, grieving, and so on.

People will readily talk about change - from the newest laptop to your promotion. They often balk at even acknowledging - let alone discussing - transition. They don't want to talk about loss or giving something up, much less deal with difficult feelings associated with letting go of old habits, old identities, even old ways of being. They will say instead, "Let's stay focused on the future. Let's move on."

Ignoring the dynamics of transition, however, doesn't mean people don't go through the process. Denial drives it underground. As Bridges says in his best-selling book, *Managing Transition*, "Under good conditions, employees spend 5-10% of their time and energy on the changes that affect them. Under more difficult conditions, they can easily spend half their time and energy that way."

That's a key point for you as you begin to manage one or more friendcos.

Understanding what happens during personal transition will be helpful as you reshape relationships with friendcos. Because it happens whether you address it consciously or not - it will take longer, and often turn out rather badly, if you ignore that elephant.

If you manage transition well, you *and* your friendcos will create a new beginning feeling stronger, more appreciative of one another, and engaged with each other in an effective way.

How does transition work?

There are three stages:

1. Endings and letting go
2. The neutral zone
3. New beginnings

What's ending? As you start managing friendcos, what will you have to let go?

You'll have to stop thinking of your friend as your peer. In the workplace, you are no longer equals. Your job now includes directing, monitoring, and even correcting the performance of your friend.

You may have to give up (or curtail) socializing with your friend after work. Even if you do continue to socialize, you'll have to give up speaking openly about what's going on at work while socializing.

You will have to give up spending as much time together at work. Far fewer lunches, for instance.

You will have to give up being "partners in crime," commiserating about the perceived troubles in the organization, if you did that sort of thing when you were co-workers.

You will have to give up using your friendco as a sounding board.

You will have to give up confiding in your friend about other people in the department or organization.

What will your friendco have to give up?

The list is similar. Your friend or former co-worker will have to let go of thinking of the two of you as peers.

- They'll be giving up spending as much time together (at work or after work).

- They may have to let go of the hope of getting the promotion that went to you.

- Your friendco may have to let go of a mentoring relationship he, or she, had with the previous manager.

- Your friendco might also have to let go of things you know nothing about.

Keys to dealing with endings and letting go

There are several things you can do to help your yourself *and* your friend or former peer navigate the white water of transition. During this first stage of transition, you can:

- Understand and **acknowledge what's being lost** (for each of you).

- Help one another **find ways to "grieve" the losses**, if necessary.

- Clearly **define what's over** - and what isn't.

- Find ways to **acknowledge the past**, not ignore or deny it.

- Create a way to "officially" **mark the ending**.

In the next chapter, we'll examine how to have a conversation *with* your friendcos to facilitate this inner game of transition. To do that effectively, you also need to understand the other two stages of the process - the Neutral Zone and New Beginnings.

The Neutral Zone

There's a space between letting go and completing your transition called the *Neutral Zone*. This can be brief, or it may take a while. Everyone, and every transition, is different.

If you were playing baseball, and decided to steal second base, there would come a moment after you sped away from first base - but before you reached second - when you would be in that zone. You're in the Neutral Zone when you realize that you can't go back, but you're not "there" yet. You're somewhere in the middle. A thought may cross your mind as you're running down the baseline - *Am I going to make it? Should I have stayed where I was safe?* Too late now - you're committed. You can't go back; you must keep going.

For most transitions, the Neutral Zone is much longer than the split second during a base stealing attempt. When you're there, likely you'll feel anxious, uncomfortable, confused, or awkward. You've begun to accept that the *past* is gone, but a landing in the *future* has yet to occur.

The Neutral Zone isn't all bad news. It's also a time when people often discover they can be creative. Because things are in flux, they start to see opportunities to rearrange things, to see the situation in a different light, to make new choices and commitments before settling into the New Beginning.

In short, the Neutral Zone is a time for both anxiety and innovation.

During this period, you might feel anxious about whether this redefined relationship is actually going to work out. You might still be feeling awkward about being in charge, and your friendco might be still unsure about having you as their boss. You might also have fresh insight and appreciation for aspects of character (yours or theirs) which were hidden until the change revealed them.

The mental act of letting go of the way things were can unleash a flood of new ideas about the way things can be.

Keys to moving through the Neutral Zone:

- **Explain that it's normal** - even predictable - to enter the Neutral Zone. Ironically, things can be less awkward if we know they're going to be awkward.

- **Encourage creative thinking**, experimentation and risk-taking.

- **Avoid pushing too soon** for closure and certainty. Ride the wave.

The New Beginning

As the transition runs its course, eventually you'll find yourself in the third stage, simply called the *New Beginning*. You are no longer "trying on" the idea that you're the leader of the team, and you are no longer wondering how you'll handle the issue of managing friends and former peers. As they enter their own new beginning, they will no longer be confused, anxious, or unsure about how to deal with you as their boss.

Keys for the New Beginning

- **Be consistent**. There will still be times when you (or they) will be tempted to fall into the old relationship patterns. Resist those temptations!

- **Recognize and reward** these folks for the work they've put into adapting to the change. Notice it and comment on it.

- Finally, find a way to **celebrate the new beginning.** Remember, these changes occurred in a larger context. It wasn't just you and your friends and former peers who've made a transition - it's the entire team. When it's become clear that you are no longer the "new" leader, and everyone has settled into the "way things are," acknowledge it and celebrate.

You now know *why* it's critical to be proactive with your friendco relationships. Doing so fosters *supportive* relationships, while ignoring the issues could create *saboteurs*.

You also know it's not enough to manage the external *change* regarding your promotion. It's imperative to deal with the internal *transition* you and your friendcos will make.

CHAPTER TWO

Ready...Aim...Manage!

Let's imagine you've been put in charge of a newly configured department comprised of seven or eight employees. One of these people, Lisa, has been a personal friend and, until now, a peer for a couple of years. You and Lisa have shared many experiences over the years, good times and bad. She's been a confidant, a shoulder to lean on, a cheerleader, and someone you could turn to when you needed to vent. The reverse is also true.

Now you're going to be her manager and you're uncomfortable because you don't know how this will impact your friendship.

Another member of the team, Scott, was a co-worker and peer in your previous department. You've worked closely with Scott on several projects, one of which was completed just last month. Scott is gregarious, open, and often peppers his conversation with good-natured humor. He's been fun to work with.

He left a voice mail to congratulate you after your promotion was announced. "I'm so happy to hear you're going to be the new manager," he said in part. "It's going to be a lot of work putting a new team together. I'm looking forward to being part of it. As for me, I'm glad *you're* going to be the new boss - I've always believed it's not who you are, it's who you know."

You have heard a rumor that Scott had been hoping for a promotion into management and *may* be resentful of your selection, but you have not spoken directly with him about this.

Rounding out the team are Jayne, Alicia, Amanda, Jose and James. Because they came from other departments, you don't know these people well, and have formed no firm opinion of them yet.

As the incoming and newly appointed manager, you'll be juggling many things: building a team from the ground up, establishing goals and objectives, assigning tasks and projects to team members, getting started with your new boss, and many others. We're going to focus here on just one of the many things on your mind: *managing your friendcos*. There will be two under your wing - your friend Lisa and your former peer Scott. To start managing them, you need a plan!

There are six elements of a good plan to begin to manage your friendcos:

1. Be prepared.

2. Have a separate, private, confidential, one-on-one conversations with Lisa and Scott.

3. Have a team meeting to broadly clarify how you will be treating all employees. (Hint: they know you're friends with Lisa and have worked with Scott. They'll be curious how you're going to deal with that.)

4. Walk the talk. Once you establish new groundrules for these two relationships, you must stick to them.

5. Check in with Lisa and Scott as needed during the transition process.

6. Find a way to acknowledge and celebrate the new beginning.

Before you talk with Lisa or Scott, I encourage you to spend some time getting ready. If the biggest mistake is to avoid these conversations altogether, the second-biggest has to be diving into them without being prepared. You should know what *outcome* you're hoping to achieve, *what* you want to say, and *how* you're going to say it.

What outcome do you want to achieve?

While your plan is principally about establishing (or changing) the ground rules of your friendco relationships going forward, there's more to it than that.

It's essential to be clear with friendcos about these new ground rules, and, as mentioned above, *it's equally important to the rest of the team*. One of the prime reasons you'll be talking with Lisa and Scott, for instance, is because you'll want to be an *impartial* manager who won't be accused of favoritism. *There are few things that will impact team morale more quickly than having some employees believe you're favoring others.* It's a foolproof recipe to turn supporters into saboteurs.

There are other outcomes which may be important to you as well. Make a list of the outcomes you want for each specific conversation you'll have:

- Establishing your credibility as the team leader.
- Reducing or eliminating the charge of favoritism.
- Cleaning up any issues you currently have with this person.
- Modeling open, frank communication with staff.
- Reducing the possibility of misunderstandings with this person that might otherwise occur.

- Improving morale or increasing their commitment to the job.
- Other outcomes unique to your situation.

What you want to say...

There are many messages you might want to include in your conversations with friendcos. Some you may want to include:

- You have new responsibilities, and you're serious about them.
- You have no apologies about your new position.
- You believe it's important to set new ground rules for any friends, co-workers, or former peers you now supervise.
- You will be keeping a professional distance and spending less time at work with this person.
- You may be, or will be spending less time with this person outside of work.
- You will be finding a new sounding board and won't be sharing confidential information with them - unless it pertains to them.
- Your decisions going forward will be based on job performance, not any relationship you've had with the person before you became the manager.

- You want and expect your decisions to be accepted without resentment, even if or when they include criticism or discipline.
- You want their commitment and active support.
- Others messages unique to your situation.

How to say it...

First, the obvious.

You're going to have a face-to-face conversation with Lisa and another with Scott. This isn't something to handle by email or a phone chat.

Did you know that some communication experts believe that only 7% of the meaning in a conversation is derived from the actual words? The rest, they say, comes from *how* it's said - the body language, the tone, the eye contact, and other non-verbal cues including the setting for the conversation.

Here are some general guidelines for your friendco conversations:

- Find a time and place that's private and comfortable. You *might* use your office, but another option is to have the conversation off-campus, so to speak, perhaps over lunch or at a coffee shop.

· Begin the conversation by being clear what you want to explore together, including what outcome(s) you want to achieve.

· To encourage their candid participation, be willing to self-disclose your own concerns, doubts, and hopes. For instance, admit your own discomfort, if any, early in the conversation.

· Speak *your* truth, but don't package it as *the* truth.

· Think of the conversation as having three parts:

   » You mostly talk.

   » You mostly listen.

   » The two of you engage in creative dialogue.

· Be an *active* listener. Paraphrase or summarize what you're hearing from time to time and check for clarity.

· After you have each shared your own truth, work together to create agreements on how to move forward.

In the next two chapters, we'll see how your conversations could unfold with Lisa and Scott.

CHAPTER FOUR

Start Managing Lisa, Your Friend

L et's start with Lisa. She's been your friend for years, both socially and at work. A couple of years ago she was hired to work in your department, and since then you've been peers doing essentially the same job. Occasionally, you have worked more closely on special projects.

Lisa was not interested in the management position you now hold, but she was delighted you were chosen. She's told you she *knows* you're going to do well.

You're not concerned about Lisa's professionalism and performance. You have no reason to doubt she'll continue to do well in her position.

Even so, it's hard to embrace the idea of becoming her boss. You worry that because she's your friend, you'll give her more time and attention than the others. You can easily see yourself turning to her for advice - old habits are hard to break. On the other hand, perhaps you should go the other way - making a point to avoid her, to minimize the perception of favoritism.

In any case, you don't want to end to your friendship.

You've decided to have a frank conversation with her as soon as possible. In thinking about the outcomes you'd like to create, you want to:

· Have both of you understand and accept your new role.

· Problem-solve together to minimize the potential for favoritism.

· Maintain your friendship, even as you modify it to accommodate the shift in authority.

You've chosen to have dinner together at a restaurant you both enjoy, because it's away from workplace distractions. Here's how the conversation might unfold:

You: Lisa, I'm glad we could spend some private time together before I get too involved in my new job.

Lisa: Me too! I'm so excited for you. You're going to be a fantastic manager. I'm just glad it's you and not me. I wouldn't take that job for anything in the world. I know myself well enough to know I don't need *those* headaches.

You: It's going to be quite a challenge, that's for sure. One of the reasons I wanted to talk, Lisa, was because... well, because we've been such good friends for such a long time, and I'd hate to think that my new job would somehow come between us.

Lisa: What do you mean? How could that happen?

You: Well, let me share a couple of things that are worrisome to me. First of all, I'm likely to feel a bit awkward at first, being your boss.

To speak plainly, I'm now your boss. At work, we're not peers anymore. I'm sure we can make all the necessary adjustments in time, but I don't want you to think I take this lightly.

Lisa: Okay, I can see that, I guess. But not to worry - we know each other too well to let something like that get out of hand.

You: Thanks. I appreciate you saying that. Let me share something else with you. I guess I feel a bit uncomfortable about "managing a friend" because I worry that there could be an issue of favoritism - or even what I'd have to call "reverse favoritism."

Lisa: Reverse favoritism? That's a new one! Please - explain!

You: Here's the thing. As a manager - even a new one - I know that I can't play favorites. I must treat everyone on the staff equally. You get that, right?

Lisa: Of course.

You: So I must be particularly careful with you, precisely because you are my friend. Neither of us can afford to have other team members think I favor you in any way. I worry that I might do that without even thinking - or - and here comes the "reverse favoritism" part - I might go out of my way to avoid you, ignore you, or give you the assignments nobody wants, just to "prove" to the staff that I'm not favoring you.

Lisa: Ah, I see. That makes sense. Well, I certainly don't want to be your pet employee - and I don't want all the lousy assignments, either. At the same time, I don't want to be walking on eggshells, afraid that I'm somehow helping to create a perception of favoritism!

You: Well, I have a couple of ideas how we can resolve this - and I'd love to hear any you might have as well. First of all, we're going to have to accept some new groundrules for our personal and professional relationship. For example, I'm not going to be able to go to lunch with you as often as before - no more than anyone else on the staff. I'll miss that but it has to be that way.

Two, although it will be tempting, I'm not going to be able to use you as a sounding board any more about work-related issues. I've always treasured your advice but it wouldn't be appropriate now. Not to mention if I shared work-related confidences with you, I'd be putting you in an awkward situation with the others. That make sense to you?

Lisa: Yes, I guess that's logical.

You: Can you say a little more about that? It sounds like you get it intellectually, but I'm wondering if you can tell me how you *feel* about it?

Lisa: Well, I guess I'm feeling a little sad. We've had such a good friendship for so long now. I understand that it has to change, but I'm going to miss the way things were. I understand that you can't share confidential information with me given your new position - I really do. And it's not even that I *want* to know all that stuff.

But it never occurred to me how much things would have to change if you got this job. And now that we're talking about it, I'm already feeling little pangs of longing for the way we used to be.

You: I know what you mean. Sometimes, people can get so excited about changes that they forget that with change comes with a price - to adapt to the new, we have to let go of the old. I too have mixed feelings. I'm very happy to have this new job, but I'm not sure I'm ready to let go of old familiar patterns!

Lisa: Yep. But everything changes eventually, right? And we've been through other things together and did just fine. There's no reason we can't make this work.

You: Thank you for saying that, Lisa. It sounds like we both understand what's at stake and how things are going to evolve. I'm glad we're having this talk.

Lisa: Me too. So, is there anything else?

You: Well, just one more thing. There is something else I feel compelled to bring up that we should both understand. I might find it necessary to spend less social time with you outside of work. I'm not convinced that's going to happen, but it might.

Lisa: I hope it doesn't come to that! I want you to do well in this job, of course - but I'd *hate* the idea of completely losing you as a friend.

You: I agree. Let's play it by ear for now. I'll let you know if I'm feeling uncomfortable, and hope you'll do the same with me.

Lisa: I can do that. I *will* do that. Anything else?

You: Actually, there is one final thing. Maybe it's related to the favoritism thing, but I think it needs to be said out loud in any case. I'm going to be making decisions in the future based on your work performance, and I can't make them based on our friendship. You might not always agree with those decisions, but I need you to accept and implement them with professionalism, just as you would for any other manager.

Lisa: Whoa! You sound so serious! What happened to my friend? Did this job go to your head already?

You: I know, I know. It's awkward just saying it. But if we talk about it now, make it clear beforehand, we might avoid an even more awkward situation later. I need to know I can count on your commitment to making this new relationship work. I also know that if the situation were reversed, you'd be asking the same of me.

Lisa: Hadn't thought about it that way - but you're right. And I meant it when I said I was excited that you got the job. I really *do* want you to succeed at it. So yes, you have my promise that I'll do my part to accept you as my boss, not just my friend, and you have my full support.

You: Can you think of anything else we should do to make this whole thing work?

Lisa: Well, now that you ask, there is one thing. You and I know we're having this little talk. But what about the rest of the staff? Aren't they already going to leap to the conclusion that I'm bound to be a favorite? They know we're friends. Would you be willing to give some version of this little speech to the rest of the staff?

You: It sounds like you're concerned that if we keep this conversation just between the two of use, you might be put on the spot with the others - or that they'll make assumptions that aren't true. Have I got that right?

Lisa: That's it in a nutshell!

You: How about I bring it up at the next staff meeting. Not with a blow-by-blow account of this conversation, but just to let everyone know I'm committed to being fair and treating everyone equally. Does that work for you?

Lisa: Yep. I would definitely appreciate that.

You: Is there anything else you'd like to bring up about any of this?

Lisa: Not particularly, I suppose. Well, there is one thing on my mind right now I *have* to bring up.

You: Yes?

Lisa: Can we order now? I'm starved!!

While your mileage will vary, you can have conversations like this one with the friends you now manage. What's required is your willingness to:

· Self-disclose and admit your own thoughts and feelings
· Assert that you take your new job seriously

- Clarify the outcomes you're seeking
- Describe the new groundrules
- Listen until you become clear about your friend's perspective
- Be empathetic as you talk about the losses and what each of you is giving up
- Work together to craft and agree on the next steps in the relationship

The *most* important thing you can do is *have the conversation*. If it doesn't go perfectly, have another one. Keep the lines of communication open and candid.

CHAPTER FIVE

Start Managing Scott, a Former Co-Worker

Unlike Lisa, Scott is not a personal friend with whom you socialize outside work. He's been a co-worker until now, and he'll be a member of your new team. You're familiar with his work, and think of him as easy-going, hard working, and fun.

You're still thinking about the voice mail he left you after word of your promotion got out. "I'm so happy you're going to be the new manager," he had said. "It's going to be a lot of work putting a new team together. I'm looking forward to being part of it. As for me, I'm glad *you're* going to be the new boss - I've always believed it's not who you are, it's who you know."

You hadn't found the time to return that phone call, but you've been wondering about it ever since. Was Scott implying anything? Does he want to somehow leverage his peer-to-peer relationship with you? Or was it just light-hearted humor?

You remember someone saying they had thought Scott had been interested in the promotion that went to you. You had the impression that he *might* be resentful of your selection, although you've never spoken with him about it.

Whether Scott wanted your new job, or is resentful of your selection, he *is* a former peer - a friendco - and you've decided to have some conversation with him as soon as possible.

The outcomes you'd like to create with Scott include:

- Establishing your credibility as the leader.
- Eliminating any perception of favoritism.
- Exploring whether Scott has any issues that need to be addressed.
- Keeping him motivated and committed to high performance.

There are several key points you want to cover with Scott:

- You have no apologies about your new position.
- You are serious about your new responsibilities.

- You will be establishing ground rules for any friends, co-workers, or former peers you now supervise.

- As manager, you will be keeping a professional distance and spending less time at work with Scott than you have in the past.

- Your decisions going forward will be based on job performance, not any relationship you've had with the person before you became the manager.

- You want Scott's commitment and active support.

Meeting with Scott for dinner as you did with Lisa would be inappropriate, given you weren't social friends, and would send a mixed signal by elevating the setting. You ask him to join you for coffee before work, to ensure your conversation is private and uninterrupted.

Here's how the conversation unfolds:

You: Thank you for meeting with me this morning, Scott. I wanted the opportunity to speak with you for a few minutes before we both got busy with our day.

Scott: Sure, boss! What's on your mind?

Managing Friends & Former Peers

You: Well, there's something I've been giving some thought as I get ready to start in my new position. It has to do with how awkward it can be sometimes for people to begin supervising people that have been their co-worker until then. I have to admit it felt a little odd at first to think of myself as your supervisor, and I wondered if perhaps you had thought about that as well.

Scott: I'm not too worried about it, to tell you the truth. I know you, and I'm sure you'll be a good manager, once you get the hang of it. Bit surprised to hear that you were offered the position, I must say. You haven't ever mentioned something like this to me before, so I didn't see it coming. This is your first management job, right?

You: Actually, it's not quite my first experience, but it's pretty close. I did supervise a couple of administrative assistants and one or two temps with a different organization a few years ago.

Although I may be new to this position, I'm confident I can handle it. I know the technical stuff pretty well as you know, and it looks like this is going to be a strong team, knowing you and Lisa as well as I do, and from what I hear about the others.

Scott: I'll tell you one thing - you'll be a much better boss than your predecessor!

You: What makes you say that?

Scott: She was never around! I could go for days without seeing her. I always felt out of the loop. But now that you're in charge, I know I'll be kept informed. We've worked so closely together that I don't have to prove myself to stay in your good graces. Like I think I told you, I've always believed it's not who you are, it's who you know!

You: Let me say a couple of things about that. First, I hope my management style will be one in which *everyone* feels like they're "in the loop." If you ever start to feel like I'm avoiding you or giving you too much independence, I hope you'll let me know. I once heard a great definition for the perfect manager: one who is hands-on as much as needed, and hands-off as much as possible. That's the philosophy I hope to practice.

That said, I don't completely agree with your comment about it not being who you are, but rather who you know. At least in terms of how I want to manage, it's more about how you perform that makes all the difference. I'm going to be making decisions based on your performance - not on our history of working together. Does that make sense?

Scott: Well, um, yeah, I hear what you're saying. But again - not to worry! You know I've got a great track record and I don't intend to get off track now.

You: Excellent. I'll hold you to that! And just to be clear, one of the things that will change between us is that I'm not going to be able to spend as much time doing things like taking lunch together as we did in the past. Doesn't mean we *won't* be having lunch now and then, but I must be sensitive to the issue of perceived favoritism.

The rest of the new team know I've worked with you for some time, and there may be those who think I'll be favoring you by giving you the best assignments, or letting you bend the rules, - you know what I mean. Perception is everything. People will form their own judgment of that issue, but I won't contribute to it by giving them reasons to think so.

Scott: Yes, I see what you mean. So it sounds like you're telling me that you're going to be treating me just like everyone else. Even with our successful working experience together.

You: If you mean I'm going to treat everyone equally and fairly, yes, that is true. If you're worried that I'm going to ignore the talent, expertise and track record you bring to the job, then let me reassure you. I'm *delighted* you're a member of the team; I'm committed to helping you be successful, and I'm going to count on your professionalism from day one.

Scott: Thank you for saying that. You see? I *knew* you were a good choice for this job!

You: So let me summarize where we are. I've acknowledged that it may be a bit strange at first with me being your boss and you reporting to me. We've agreed that it's my job to be fair with everyone on the team and treat them all as equally as I can. I've told you I'm going to try to be as hands-on as anyone on the team needs me to be, while being as hands-off as possible. And you seem to be saying you will commit to keeping your professional work standards *and* give me your full support as the manager. Have I got it right?

Scott: That's a great summary, boss. You're the new Fearless Leader, and I've got your back. Works for me.

You: Very funny. Whoa! Look at the time. We'd better get to the office!

CHAPTER SIX

The Road Ahead

The truth is there should be no difference between managing friendcos and managing anyone else, except that you should begin that supervision by establishing new ground rules for these unique relationships.

As we've seen, the effort starts with a solid plan, which consists of six elements:

1. Prepare for the initial conversation with each friendco, by deciding what outcome you want to achieve, what you want to say, and how you're going to say it.

2. Have these private conversations, agreeing to the appropriate new ground rules.

3. Hold a team meeting to establish your credibility as the new leader, addressing head-on the issue of favoritism (given that everyone knows you have friendcos on the team).

4. Begin managing the team, treating everyone fairly and equally.

5. Check in with friendcos as needed during the first few weeks to help with their transition process.

6. As the team becomes established as "your" team, find ways to acknowledge and celebrate the team's cohesion and achievements.

Of course, one conversation to establish new ground rules may not completely put the matter to rest. It's quite conceivable that a friendco could ask you to cut them some slack when a situation arises in the future.

For instance, a friendco could start coming to work late. After two or three instances, you decide to have a conversation to see what's going on and put an end to it. They explain that they have child care issues; the usual sitter quit suddenly, and the back-up plan (calling on the mother-in-law) hasn't quite worked out yet.

They ask for your understanding and ask that you look the other way for a short time while they sort it out. After all, they say, you know them, and you now know the problem. You know how difficult it is to find another sitter.

The problem - *your problem* - is that you need this person to come to work on time, friendco or otherwise.

This is where you might find it best to hear yourself saying something like this:

"I do understand and appreciate what you're going through. If I was wearing my "friend" hat, I'd want to give you as much time as possible to resolve this. But, I have to put on my "manager" hat now. Just as I need every other employee to come to work on time, I need *you* to do the same. Our policy is... (describe the policy). I know it's a tough situation, but unless you can be at work on time, I have no choice but to take the next step in the disciplinary process."

While this may be uncomfortable, it's really no different from having to talk to any employee about a performance shortfall which could lead to discipline. It's a part of being a manager.

What else can you do?

Beyond having a basic plan, there are many other things you can do to effectively supervise a team with friendcos. You can get a mentor, from within or outside the organization. Actually, this is sound advice for anyone in a leadership role, no matter how green or seasoned they may be.

Since it's highly inappropriate - and generally poor practice - to turn to a subordinate for suggestions on how to handle another subordinate, having a mentor gives you the opportunity to think "out loud," without having to worry about how the team will react to your thoughts.

If you haven't already begun a habitual reading regimen, get started now. Commit to reading something about management or leadership every single week. It's no different from hitting the gym on a regular basis - except you don't have to share equipment or change clothes in a sweaty locker room. It's exercise for your brain. There are countless books, journals, articles, and blogs which will enrich your leadership practice with insight and examples of proven techniques out there. Find them, and read them.

When you can, enroll in public or in-house leadership and management development programs. While this book puts a microscope on *one* leadership challenge, its mission is to enhance, not replace, formal training. Don't hesitate to enroll in something at least once a year. It's a valuable use of time - you'll get the chance to mingle with other participants who face similar challenges as you, learn (and practice) new skills, and come back to the job with a fresh perspective and a recharged attitude.

Do not fear supervising friends and former co-workers. Accept the challenge, and frame it as an opportunity to become a strong, effective leader. As Stephen Covey has said, "Opposition is a natural part of life. Just as we develop our physical muscles by overcoming opposition - such as lifting weights - we develop our character muscles by overcoming challenges and adversity."

Meeting the challenge of supervising friendcos is a powerful way to develop your leadership muscles.

Don't hesitate. Start creating your plan today.

*M*anaging *Friends & Former Peers* is the first in what will be an ever-expanding collection of *Just In Time* books. Each will focus on just one issue, and provide insight, techniques, and practical solutions for that issue.

Available right now:

So, How Was Your Meeting?
TIPS* on conducting effective meetings.

Managing the Soon to Retire Employee
TIPS* on dealing with "Sooners" – employees who will be retiring within three years or less.

Coming soon:

Making Waves
TIPS* on how to introduce change in your workplace.

Taking the Guesswork out of Teamwork

TIPS* on the most important things you can do to create a cohesive, highly productive team.

Give 'em the Kool Aid!

TIPS* on crafting mission or purpose statements that rock to create alignment and team commitment

When You've Just Been Put in Charge

TIPS* on the critical first steps to take to manage your transition into a new leadership role.

Setting Expectations, Standards and Goals

TIPS* on how to make sure your expectations are clear, how to establish appropriate standards, and set "sweet-spot" goals: optimistic and realistic

Lean Into Your Discomfort Without Falling on Your Face

TIPS* on the impact of ground rules, norms and unspoken agreements within your team.

What Got You to the Party May Get You Shown to the Door

TIPS* on why the skill sets that you leveraged for a promotion may need to be broadened to succeed in management. What are the most critical skills will you need to be successful in your new role?

"What Flows Down; "How Flows Up

TIPS* to help you avoid micro-managing your team. Great leaders are hands-off as much as possible, and hands-on as much as needed. How do you do *that*?

Fabulous Feedback -

TIPS* on how to give people powerful feedback which actually results in changed behavior and renewed commitment

TIPS = Techniques, Insight, and Practical Solutions

Made in the USA
Columbia, SC
12 February 2021

32799848R00046